Children's Word Games and Crossword Puzzles

For Ages 9 and Above
Edited by Eugene T. Maleska

TIMES
T
BOOKS

Library of Congress Cataloging-in-Publication Data
Maleska, Eugene T.
    Children's word games and crossword puzzles.
    Summary: A collection of original crossword puzzles
and word games for players aged nine and up.
    1. Crossword puzzles—Juvenile literature. 2. Word
games—Juvenile literature. [1. Crossword puzzles.
2. Word games] I. Maleska, Eugene T.
GV1507.C7C44 1986   793.73′2   86-886
ISBN 0-8129-1308-6

Manufactured in the United States of America

2468B97531

Woodcut illustrations by Lars and Lois Hokanson

1.
House of Words

by Louis Sabin

This is a small house. But inside, it is large enough for thirteen words, of one, two, three, and four letters. How many can you make from the letters A, B, C, D, and E? Use a letter only once in each word. Do not use names, abbreviations, slang, or foreign words.

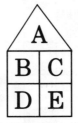

We added an extra room. Now the house looks like this. How many more words can you make, using the new letter with the other four? We found seven new words.

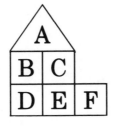

2.
Disneyland Characters

by Louis Sabin

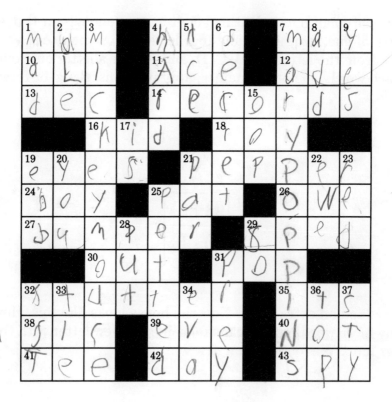

The completed crossword grid contains handwritten answers:

1M	2a	3M		4h	5t	6s		7m	8a	9y
10a	L	i		11A	c	e		12o	d	e
13d	e	c		14r	e	c	15o	r	d	s
		16k	17i	d		18t	o	y		
19e	20y	e	s		21p	e	p	p	22e	23r
24b	o	y		25p	a	t		26o	W	e
27d	u	n	28p	e	r		29g	p	e	d
		30o	u	t		31p	o	p		
32s	33t	u	t	34e	r		35t	i	36t	37s
38s	i	r		39e	v	e		40N	o	t
41T	e	e		42d	a	y		43s	p	y

Across

1 A parent's nickname

4 "He put in ___ thumb . . ."

7 Month after April

10 Muhammad ___, retired boxer

11 Highest playing card

12 Orange or lemon drink

13 Month after Nov. (Abbreviation)

14 Phonograph platters

16 Young goat; young guy

18 Cowboy ___ Rogers

19 What we see with

21 Salt's table partner

24 Young man

25 _____ Boone is a famous singer

26 If you use a credit card, you _____ money

27 Car's protective bar, often having a sticker

29 Ran; hurried

30 Go _____ (leave the house)

31 *Hop on* _____: Dr. Seuss book

32 Speak like Porky Pig

35 Word that's short for "it is"

38 Bro's relative

39 Mother of Cain and Abel

40 "Ready or _____, here I come!"

41 Tiny gadget for a golfer

42 It follows night

43 The British hanged Nathan Hale because he was a _____

Down

1 Crazy or very angry

2 Cheer, at a bullfight

3 Walt Disney's squeaky cartoon character: 2 words

4 Difficult; tough

5 Frozen water

6 Something to keep and never tell

7 Walt Disney's "flying nanny," played by Julie Andrews: 2 words

8 Do this to 2 and 2, to get 4

9 Okay, sure, I will

15 Alley _____: cartoon character

17 Albany _____ the capital of New York

19 Go away from shore, like the tide

20 "_____ Can't Do That" is a Beatles song

21 What golfers hope to shoot

22 Lamb's mother

23 Apple color

25 Caressed a dog or cat

28 "Polly _____ the kettle on"

29 "You Are _____ Beautiful" is a popular song

31 Any animal tracked by a hunter

32 Fast-flying plane

33 Piece of clothing to make a knot in

34 Little _____, girl in *Uncle Tom's Cabin*

36 Spinning toy

37 Pigpen

3.
Cross-Words

by Peter G. Snow

A	P	E		S	I	R		A	N	T
S	I	X		A	R	E		T	O	N
P	E	P		M	I	S	T	E	R	T
		L	O	O	S	E	R			
L	E	A	R	N		T	I	M	I	D
E	R	I	E			H	A	L	E	
G	A	N	G	S		G	I	R	L	S
		O	P	E	R	A	S			
G	R	A	N	O	L	A		H	A	M
O	I	L		M	I	S	T	A	G	E
O	D	E		L	E	E		L	O	T

Across

1 Swinger in a jungle

4 Title for a knight

7 Insect that lives in a hill

10 Average age of a first-grader

11 Anger

12 2,000 pounds

13 Vigor

14 *A-Team* character: 2 words

16 Less tight

18 What you do in school if you pay attention

20 Shy

24 One of the Great Lakes

25 What some poets call a valley

26 Groups of criminals

28 Young women

29 Plays set to music

31 Breakfast cereal

34 Meat from a pig

37 Petroleum

38 Suffix with arson or violin

39 Grow older

40 Type of poem

41 Leader of the Confederate Army

42 Parcel of land

Down

1 Type of snake that killed Cleopatra

2 Lemon meringue ____

3 Make understandable

4 An apostle named Peter

5 Flower or eye part

6 Fix a broken bone a second time

7 Had lunch

8 Word often used with neither

9 Powerful explosive

15 Unimportant matters

17 State north of California

18 This is between your hip and your foot

19 A distinctive period, sometimes called an age

21 Lawman of the Old West

22 Sick

23 ____ Moines (capital of Iowa)

27 Damage or destroy

28 Fireplace

30 Other or otherwise

31 Sticky stuff

32 Gardeners try to get ____ of weeds

33 Drink that sounds like "ail"

35 Dinosaurs roamed the Earth long ____

36 Was introduced to

4.
My! My!
by Merryl Maleska

Using the definitions, fill in the missing letters and also fill in the puzzle.

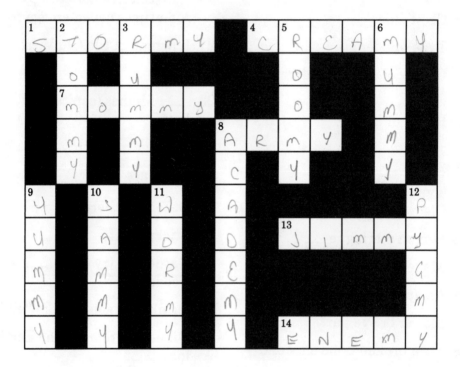

Across

1 When it rains and the wind blows hard, it's ____ weather

S T O R MY

4 Some pies and the top part of a carton of milk are very

____

_ _ _ _ MY

7 This is a nickname for a child's mother

_ _ _ MY

8 Soldiers are men in the ___   _ _ MY

13 ___ Carter was the U.S.
president before Ronald
Reagan   _ _ _ MY

14 When someone hates you
and wants to hurt you, he is
your ___   _ _ _ MY

Down

2 "Little ___ Tucker sang for
his supper"   _ _ _ MY

3 What card game is
sometimes called gin?   _ _ _ MY

5 When a house has lots of
space, it is ___   _ _ _ MY

6 King Tut is a famous ___
in Egypt   _ _ _ MY

8 The United States Military
___ is in West Point, New
York   _ _ _ _ _ MY

9 When you eat something
you like very much, what do
you say?   _ _ _ MY

10 ___ Davis, Jr., is a famous
singer and actor and dancer   _ _ _ MY

11 If an apple has a hole in it,
then it might be ___   _ _ _ MY

12 A very small person who
lives in Africa is called a
___   _ _ _ MY

5.
Sweets
by Caroline G. Fitzgerald

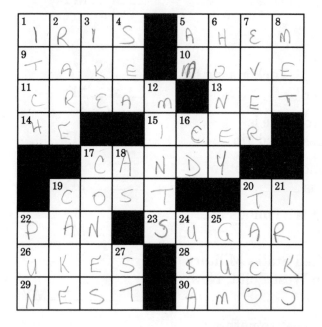

Across

1 Spring flower with a beard

5 Cough-like sound for attention

9 Opposite of give

10 Take a turn in checkers

11 Ice ____ is sold at amusement parks

13 Tennis-court divider

14 "And a merry old soul was ____"

15 Person who puts the frosting on the pastry

17 Fudge or taffy

19 Price

20 La, ____, do

22 You cook food in this

23 This makes sweets sweet

26 Ukuleles, for short

28 How to eat a lollipop

29 Bird's home

30 ___ and Andy

Down

1 Something to scratch

2 Like a pink steak

3 Pres. Eisenhower's nickname

4 Ocean

5 "What a good boy ___ I!"

6 Sweet made by a bee

7 "...lived happily ___ after."

8 "Simple Simon ___ a pieman..."

12 After-dinner candies

16 Letters between B and E

17 Holders for 11 Across

18 "Stay as Sweet ___ You Are" (old song)

19 Angel or devil's food, for example

20 Tortilla "sandwich"

21 Annoys

22 "Canoe row a boat?" is an example of a ___

24 Bruce Springsteen wrote "Born in the ___"

25 Bubble or chewing ___

27 ___ Louis, Mo.

6.
An Hour of Fun
by Walter Covell

¹B	²A	³D		⁴W	⁵A	⁶S	
⁷E	R	A	⁸A	⁹S	¹⁰S	I	S	T	¹¹S
¹²L	E	T	¹³S	P	A	N	I	E	L
¹⁴O	N	E	¹⁵H	A	M		¹⁶D	E	E
¹⁷W	A	S	¹⁸H	E	R		¹⁹H	E	R	D
		²⁰A	S	K	²¹M	E			
²²S	²³A	²⁴L	T		²⁵L	O	N	²⁶G	²⁷E	²⁸R
²⁹A	L	A		³⁰S	I	S		³¹A	R	E
³²F	O	R	³³T	U	N	E		³⁴T	A	N
³⁵E	N	D	I	N	G	G		³⁶E	S	E
	³⁷E	S	S					³⁸S	E	N

Across

1 Like Leroy Brown

4 "There ____ a crooked man"

7 Earned run average (Abbreviation)

8 Helps

12 Allow

13 Cocker ____ (a hunting dog)

14 Six minus five

15 ____ and eggs

16 Kiki ____ is a rock star

17 Laundry appliance

19 Group of cows or horses

20 "____ no questions; I'll tell you no lies": 2 words

22 ____ and pepper

25 Extending farther

29 Pie ____ mode: 2 words

30 What son calls daughter, for short

31 "We ____ the World," famous song

32 *The Wheel of* ____, TV game show

34 Sun-browned

35 Conclusions

36 Between east and southeast (Abbreviation)

37 Nineteenth letter, or suffix for host

38 Use a needle and thread

Down

1 Under

2 Place for boxing bouts

3 June 6 and March 15, for example

4 Finish first in a race

5 Out of the way or in reserve

6 What pilots do

8 Logs after burning become ____

9 Glittering like a diamond

10 America's Uncle

11 Snow coaster

18 Head covering

19 Rooster's mother

21 He received the Ten Commandments

22 Vault for valuables

23 When you're on your own, you're ____

24 Animal fats

26 Doors for fences

27 Remove blackboard chalk marks

28 Continue a subscription that's ending

30 The cause of daylight

33 "My country, ____ of thee"

7.
Baby Talk
by Bernice Gordon

The completed crossword grid contains the following filled-in letters:

1 M	**2** A	**3** M	**4** A		**5** M	**6** A	**7** P		
8 O	V	E	R		**9** W	A	T	**10** E	**11** S
12 T	O	N	E		**13** A	N		**14** S	E
15 H	I		**16** A	G	O		**17** T	A	R
	18 D	**19** A	**20** N	C	E	R		**21** D	A
		22 R	A	T	S		**23** C	H	E
	25 R	A	M	S		**26** D	O	O	R
27 T	U	B	E		**28** C	A	L	M	
29 O	N		**30** T	A	S	T	E	**31** S	
32 A	N	**33** T		**34** A	S	H		**35** T	**36** O
37 S	E	E		**38** M	E		**39** S	H	O P
41 T	R	A	D	**42** E	S		**43** H	I	V E
		44 R	O	S			**45** E	D	E N

Across

1 One of the first words spoken by many babies

5 Picture in a geography book

8 Finished

9 Uses a hose in the garden

12 Sound of your voice or your stereo

13 "___ apple a day . . ."

14 ___ of books in a library

15 Hello!

16 Long, long ___

17 Material used in paving a road

18 Fred Astaire, or one of Santa's reindeer

21 Another of baby's first words

22 The Pied Piper's victims

23 What to do with gum

25 Farm animals that butt

26 Entrance to the house

27 Toothpaste container

28 Quiet, like the ocean

29 Opposite of off

30 Takes a sip

32 Small insect that likes to go to picnics

34 ___ tray, for cigars

35 Pussycat said: "I've been ___ London . . . "

37 "___ a pin and pick it up"

38 "Bake ___ a cake as fast as you can"

39 Go marketing

41 Swaps

43 Colony of bees

44 Stick

45 Garden in the Bible

Down

1 Night-flying insect related to a butterfly

2 Keep away from

3 Adult males

4 "These ___ a few of my favorite things . . . "

5 Large English house

6 One ___ a time

7 Nuisance

9 Payment for working

10 Schoolbook

11 What scarecrows are made of

16 Performs on the stage

19 Person living in Syria

20 ___ *That Tune*, TV program

23 Young horse

24 " . . . and the ___ of the brave"

25 Racer; sprinter

26 Fifty-yard ___

27 A breakfast food

28 Large boxes

30 Subdued, as a wild animal

31 Hot spot in the kitchen

33 Rip

36 "Do not ___ until Christmas"

39 That girl

40 Put away secretly

42 First note of the scale

8.
Noel!

by Caroline G. Fitzgerald

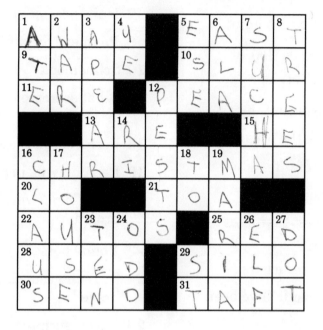

Across

1 "____ in a Manger" (a Christmas carol)

5 "They . . . saw a star shining in the ____ . . . "

9 Sticky strip to seal wrappings

10 Rhyming synonym for blur

11 "I heard him exclaim ____ they drove . . . "

12 "'____ on the earth, good will to men . . .'"

13 "We Three Kings of Orient ____" (another carol)

15 " . . . up the chimney ____ rose"

16 "The Twelve Days of ____" (another carol)

20 ____ and behold!

21 Mary "gave birth ____ son . . .": 2 words

22 Motorcars

25 Color of Rudolph's nose

28 Secondhand, as a car

29 Storage tower on a farm

30 Mail, as a Christmas card

31 The 27th U.S. president, William Howard ____

Down

1 Dined

2 Opposite of peace on earth

3 "A partridge in ____ tree": 2 words

4 "O Come, All ____ Faithful" (another carol)

5 Opposite WNW

6 Pie ____ mode: 2 words

7 "... there arose ____ clatter ...": 2 words

8 We trim these for Christmas

12 Nuisances

14 Abbreviation for the smallest state in the U.S.A.

16 "Santa ____ Is Comin' to Town"

17 "... all through the ____ / Not a creature ..."

18 "Joy ____ the World" (another carol)

19 Mary, to José

23 "____ pipers piping, nine drummers ..."

24 Eccentric or strange

26 One of Santa's helpers

27 Tiny spot

29 "Jolly Old ____ Nicholas" (Christmas song)

9.
An How!

by Louis Sabin

The letters AN are in each of the five-letter words below. There are definitions of the words next to their boxes. How many words can you fill in?

#						Definition
1	A	N	G	E	L	Heavenly being
2	A	N	N	E	X	It's formed where two lines meet
3	A	N	K	L	E	Every foot has one
4	A	N	G	E	R	Fury
5	D	A	N	C	E	A tango or a waltz
6	C	A	N	D	Y	A chocolate bar or caramel
7	P	A	N	D	A	Animal that might remind you of a teddy bear
8	C	A	N	A	L	Suez or Panama
9	S	T	A	N	D	What you must do when the national anthem is played
10			A	N		Religious song
11	G	R	A	N	D	This goes with mother, father, son, or daughter
12	P	I	A	N	O	Popular instrument with 88 keys

13	C	L	E	A	N
14	P	E	C	A	N
15	S	E	D	A	N
16	O	R	G	A	N
17	A	L	I	E	N
18	A	S	I	A	N
19	A	G	A	I	N
20	A	P	R	O	N

____ as a whistle

Kind of nut

Kind of car or chair

Instrument played in church

Foreigner

Japanese or Chinese, for instance

One more time

What a chef wears

10.
Song-and-Dance Man

by June Boggs

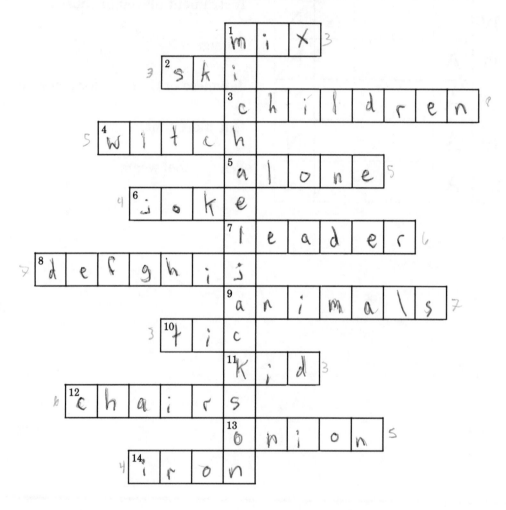

Down

1 He sings and dances. Everybody likes him. Who is it?: 2 words

Across

1 Stir together

2 People do this on a snowy hill

3 Hansel, Gretel, Tiny Tim, and others

4 Character in *The Wizard of Oz*

5 By yourself

6 What a comic tells

7 Someone to follow

8 Letters between C and K

9 What pigs and cows are

10 Word before tac and toe

11 Baby goat

12 Musical ____ is a party game

13 You might put this on a burger

14 It gets wrinkles out of clothes

11.
Riddle Square
by Mark Diehl

Circle one letter in each box from left to right to make five 5-letter words that fit the category on the right of the square. The remaining letters will answer the riddle below the square.

FG	IR	AN	DP	EI
AN	GP	OP	LN	EL
BY	EH	AR	LR	FY
AL	EW	MO	OR	MN
PT	EH	AE	CR	EH

Fruits:

Grape

Apple

Berry

Lemon

Peach

Riddle: What is worse than finding a worm in your apple?

_____

_____

22

12.
Playground Games
by Mark Diehl

1 S	2 O	3 N	4 S		5 I	6 N	7 S		8 A	9 J	10 A	11 R
12 E	D	I	T		13 N	E	T		14 S	U	R	E
15 L	O	N	E		16 T	A	R		17 A	M	E	N
18 P	R	E	G	19 Z	E	T	A	20 G		21		
			22 R	O	N		23 A	24				
25 C	26 A	27 R		28 O	D	29 D		30 S			31	32
33 A	L	E	34 S		35 S	A	36	37				
38 W	I	D	E	39 R		40 Y		41		42		
		43 R	E		44	45		46				
47 F	48 R	O		49	50 P				51	52	53	
54 L	A	V	55 A		56 O			57				
58 A	G	E	D		59 D			60				
61 W	E	R	E		62 H			63				

Across

1 Cain, Abel, and Seth were ____ of Adam and Eve

5 Opposite of outs

8 Slightly open, as a door

12 Correct before printing

13 It's in the middle of a tennis court

14 Certain about

15 The ____ Ranger

16 One part of asphalt

17 Prayer ending

(Continued)

18 Game where you stop when touched: 2 words

21 Tap lightly on the head or back

22 Name that rhymes with Don and John

23 Two of a kind

25 Part of a freight train

28 Opposite of even

30 Supermarket

33 Ginger ____ (soft drinks)

35 Uncle ____, symbol of the U.S.

37 Made a web

38 Farther across, or not so narrow

40 John Paul Jones said: "I have not ____ begun to fight"

42 It's found in a nest or in a coop

43 Bring in the crop

45 "Ready, ____, fire!"

47 To and ____ (back and forth)

49 Skipping game often played on a sidewalk or at a playground

54 Hot stuff from a volcano

56 A promise to pay (Initials)

57 Story

58 Old, like some cheese

59 This goes with neither

60 Test

61 "The Way We ____" is a popular song

62 Spin ____ Bottle is an indoor game

63 They're good for kissing

Down

1 An automat is a ____-service restaurant

2 Smell

3 Number of letters in the first month of school

4 Drive a car

5 Means to do

6 ____ and tidy

7 Belt for holding books together

8 As flat ____ pancake: 2 words

9 Double Dutch: 2 words

10 Location

11 Apartment payment

19 Animal park

20 This is sold at service stations

24 Players in a playground game

24

25 Crow's cry

26 ____ Baba fooled forty thieves

27 Game where you run when called: 2 words

29 Twenty-four hours

31 Carpet's relative

32 School subject (Abbreviation)

34 Use your eyes

36 Use a teaspoon when following a recipe

39 Cheerleader's shout

41 ____-tac-toe

44 Use your index finger

46 Vacation stop for the night

47 Mistake

48 Anger

50 Winnie the ____

51 Cab

52 Applaud with your hands

53 Stitchings at the bottoms of dresses

55 Lemony drink

13.
How Fast Are You?

by Peter G. Snow

If you can solve this puzzle in one hour, go to the head of the class!

1	2	3	4		5	6	7	8		9 r	10 e	11 d
12					13					14		
15					16					17		
			18 b	19 o y				20	21			
22 r	23 o	24 a	s	t		25 b	26 a	s e				
27 e	g	g		28	29				30	31	32	33
34				35 m	e	l	t s	36		37 r	o n
38			39	40					41 o	d	d
			42	43				44	45			
46 S	47 a	48 l	a	d			49					
50 m	a	d		51 a	52 c	53 e s			54	55	56	57
58				59					60 d	i	l l
61				62					63 y o		J K

Across

1 ____ rain is a problem in Eastern states

5 Transmit a message

9 One of the colors of the American flag

12 Went by bus or by car

13 Always

26

14 A lemon drink that sounds like "aid"

15 Pairs

16 ___ Rose is a famous baseball player

17 Exclamation of surprise

18 Container for tools

20 Pay out, as money

22 Cook in an oven

25 1st, 2nd, 3rd, or home in baseball

27 Something laid by a hen

28 Grand or majestic

30 Pleasant or polite

34 "The Bells ___ Ringing," old song

35 Thaws

37 Nickname for Ronald

38 Gnat or rat

40 In addition, or too

41 Opposite of even

42 Simple

44 British princess and former British queen

46 Dish of cold raw vegetables

49 Nickname for President Eisenhower

50 Anger

51 Cards that are better than kings

54 Cleveland's Great Lake

58 Between nine and eleven

59 Mournful sound

60 Type of pickle

61 Sorrowful

62 Type or kind

63 The yellow part of an egg

Down

1 Painting or sculpture, for example

2 "The ___ jumped over the moon"

3 Wedding promise: 2 words

4 School furniture

5 Abbreviation for a fall month

6 The night before Christmas

7 What you might use to catch a crab

8 Clothing for a girl

9 Another word for anger

10 Garden where Adam and Eve lived

11 Act or action

19 Part of a list

21 Ballpoint ___

22 Harvest

23 Fairy-tale villain

27

(Continued)

24 The Middle ___ ended about 400 years ago

25 A ___ goat is a relative of a ram

26 Pretends on the stage

29 Small green vegetables

31 A steam ___ presses clothes

32 A set of secret symbols

33 Some football players

36 Make very wet

39 What some people drink instead of coffee

43 Second president of the U.S.

45 Poor

46 Occupies a chair

47 Region

48 Opposite of borrow

49 "Money ___ everything"

52 Sound made by pigeons

53 A sound receiver in your head

55 Word used before Grande or de Janeiro

56 Sick

57 Animal with very large horns

14.
Words You Should Know

by Walter Covell

Across

1 _____ of Allegiance

5 Not loud

9 Stroke lightly

12 Pest, to a dog

13 Group of three

14 Summer drink

15 Dread

16 Fairy-tale monster

17 Religious sister

18 Some opera singers

20 Happy song

21 Nickname used by a brother

(Continued)

24 Scar on a car

25 What a movie star does

26 Unmoving

28 Door hole for mail

30 Think of respectfully

32 Pleasure boats

36 Faucet leak

38 What selfish people don't do

39 Beat harshly

42 Go by car

44 Henna is one

45 Steady, easy gait

46 Went up

48 Yes, to a senator

49 Examine closely

50 Remain

54 "There was a crooked ___"

55 Voice below soprano

56 Assistant

57 Overhead trains, for short

58 Antlered animal

59 On top of

Down

1 Light-switch position

2 Ginger ___

3 Hot or cold drink

4 Unyielding or difficult

5 Kitchen range

6 Church instruments

7 At the beginning

8 Foot part

9 Sudden terror

10 Grownup

11 Campsite shelters

19 Lazy one

20 Fastening for a door

21 Direction between SE and S

22 "___ a girl!"

23 Make a lap

27 Rocky shelf

29 Desert waterholes

31 Wonderful happening

33 Owned

34 Make an effort

35 Observe

37 Captain Kidd was one

39 Blaze

40 Faithful

41 Uncloses

43 Giver

47 Isaac's eldest son in the Bible

49 Unhappy

51 Pencil end, for instance

52 Hubbub

53 Strong wish or Japanese coin

15.
Summer Spectacle

by June Boggs

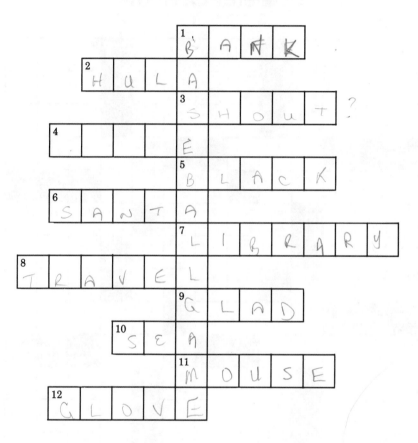

Down

1 A place to see a pitcher: 2 words

Across

1 Safe place for money

2 Hawaiian dance

3 Yell

4 Bell sound

5 Color of coal

6 Man in a red suit

7 Many books are here

8 Go on a trip

9 Happy

10 Ships travel on this

11 Mickey or Minnie

12 It keeps your hand warm

16.
Threes, Fours and Fives
by Peter G. Snow

Across

1 Sleeveless coat worn by Dracula

5 Stop

9 Nickname for President Lincoln

12 Ali Baba said: "____ sesame!"

13 One of the Great Lakes

14 "Little ____ Riding Hood"

15 Past tense of go

16 Last word in prayers

17 Game in which one player chases the others

18 Finish

20 Test the flavor of something by eating or drinking it

22 Place to buy things

25 Very large

27 2,000 pounds

28 A sloppy person, in slang

30 Garden in the Bible

34 "All men ____ created equal"

35 Name of a book or poem

37 Tool used to cut down trees

38 Relax

40 Test by touching

41 Uncooked

42 A slang term for meals

44 Stalks of plants, such as roses

46 Add up

49 Insect that makes honey

50 Expression of discovery

51 What a clock tells

54 Grows older

58 Border, as on a cup

59 The highest cards

60 Wander around

61 Part of a foot

62 What some people pay for their house or apartment

63 A meat-and-vegetables dish

Down

1 Animal that gives milk

2 Popular zoo animal; a friend of Tarzan

3 Writing tool or pig's home

4 Go in

5 Part of the body above the neck

6 Part of the body between the shoulder and hand

7 Tell a fib

8 What people might live in on camping trips

9 Nicknames for those named Arthur

10 Defeat

11 The outside part

19 Home for a raven

21 Had for supper

22 It twinkles in the sky at night

23 Ripped

24 Smallest numbers

25 What a person does on Election Day

26 Having the power or skill to do something

(Continued)

29 Raise

31 Take a risk

32 Quiz

33 What you find in the morning paper

36 Otherwise

39 A drink that might be hot or iced

43 Part of a church

45 What comes from your eyes when you are sad

46 Small jelly-filled pastry

47 Cleveland's state

48 Opposite of wild

49 The most excellent

52 Frozen water

53 Males

55 Received or obtained

56 First woman in the Bible

57 What seamstresses and tailors do

17.
Words Around the House

by Louis Sabin

The 35 words in the word list are hidden in the mixture of letters. The words can read forward or backward, up or down, or diagonally, but are always in a straight line. To complete the puzzle, locate each hidden word and draw a circle around it. A letter can appear in more than one word, so some of the circles you draw may cross or overlap. As you find the words, cross them off the list. When you have circled all of the words on the list, you have solved the puzzle.

```
T A B L E G U R T C
D E B L A D D E R A
O C L O C K P T A N
O N Y E A F O S Y E
R O N E V O T A Z N
T R O R R I M O P A
S I N K M L S T B P
T A P E R A D I O K
E H R T A M A P O I
P C O T G P U C K N
```

Bed, book, can, cane, chair, clock, cot, cup, door, foil, iron, ladder, lamp, map, mat, mirror, mop, napkin, oven, pan, pets, pot, radio, rag, rug, sink, sofa, step, table, tap, television, timer, toaster, toy, tray.

35

18.
Alphabet Starters

by Peter G. Snow

Across

1 First four letters of the alphabet

5 Next four letters of the alphabet

9 Next three letters of the alphabet

12 The back part

13 A telephone code

14 Moving truck

15 Poet Millay or author Ferber

16 Types of bread and whiskey

17 Fuss or excitement

18 Fuel for an automobile

20 Doctrine or belief

22 Twelve dozen

25 Opposite of closed

27 Male sheep

28 Nickname for Katherine

30 Small arrow

34 Grow older

35 Locations

37 Large body of water

38 Crooked

40 Nothing more than

41 Common ending for verbs

42 Initials of the world's largest nation

44 Jackets

46 Tree branch

49 "____ all in the game"

50 Mountain in Switzerland

51 Last word in a prayer

54 Soft drink

58 Name for a lion

59 Arlo Guthrie is a ____ singer

60 Very dry, like a desert

61 Comedian Rickles

62 Male cats or turkeys

63 Type of musical instrument

Down

1 Plural of "is"

2 Sleeping place

3 Is able

4 Pulls or hauls with effort

5 Organs of hearing

6 Cook in a pan

7 Exclamation of wonder often followed by "whiz"

8 This is supposed to make waste

9 Common Russian name

10 A green precious stone

11 Tie or entangle a rope or string

19 Inquires

21 The ____ (words after a movie)

22 Seize suddenly

23 Great anger

24 Something supposed to foretell the future

25 Furry water animal

26 Noble or equal

29 Points at, as a gun

31 Where India and China are located

32 Monthly housing payment

33 Labels or license plates

(Continued)

36 Religious group

39 Pull with great force

43 Part of an arrow or spear

45 Movie award

46 Lacking hair on the head

47 Butter substitute

48 "Once ＿＿ a time"

49 Writing fluids

52 Sound from a cow

53 Shade tree

55 Metal in its native state

56 Tell an untruth

57 Total up

19.
Circle the Words: Birds

by James and Phyllis Barrick

The 35 words in the word list are hidden in the mixture of letters. The words can read forward or backward, up or down, or diagonally, but are always in a straight line. To complete the puzzle, locate each hidden word and draw a circle around it. A letter can appear in more than one word, so some of the circles you draw may cross or overlap. As you find the words, cross them off the list. When you have circled all of the words on the list, you have solved the puzzle.

```
S  P  I  S  I  B  I  W  I  K  A  N  A  R  R
P  U  Q  O  P  N  O  P  A  R  R  O  T  E  W
O  H  J  O  L  R  E  A  L  M  N  I  R  E  S
O  X  E  T  R  A  A  R  T  O  M  E  L  L  N
N  K  U  A  E  H  R  A  W  N  V  G  H  R  Y
B  I  P  K  S  A  R  K  L  O  A  E  E  R  W
I  S  B  C  R  A  N  E  D  E  E  T  R  O  A
L  N  L  O  O  A  N  E  P  G  T  Y  O  O  X
L  I  N  C  R  E  L  T  H  I  E  D  N  G  W
E  W  I  M  N  T  P  W  B  P  P  I  R  N  I
R  H  O  P  R  E  H  E  O  E  M  D  R  I  N
T  I  Q  U  A  I  L  R  C  D  O  I  N  M  G
E  S  T  A  H  A  E  K  U  D  A  L  I  A  R
P  N  A  C  I  L  E  P  O  S  U  E  Q  L  S
C  R  A  S  O  R  I  O  L  E  H  U  M  F  Y
```

Auk, bittern, cockatoo, crane, dodo, eagle, flamingo, heron, ibis, kea, kiwi, meadowlark, oriole, owl, parakeet, parrot, pelican, petrel, pheasant, pigeon, plover, quail, rail, rhea, robin, sandpiper, scaup, serin, sparrow, spoonbill, thrush, turtledove, waxwing, woodpecker, wren.

20.
Birthday Party

by Caroline G. Fitzgerald

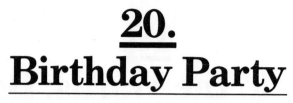

Across

1 Blind as ____ : 2 words

5 "Leave ____ alone, and they'll come home . . ."

9 "And pretty maids all ____ row": 2 words

12 Like a lemon

13 A big one delights a surfer

14 Fish or Massachusetts Cape

15 3 ____ 21 is 7

16 Unwrap a gift

17 Finish

18 "What ____ boy am I!": 2 words

20 Sons of a queen

22 Roly-____

24 Negative word, often after neither

25 Sharp, shrill bark

28 Arrest a crook

29 Where the sun sets

32 Make a boo-boo

33 Two times

36 Exclamation of pleasure

37 Stairway part

39 Cowboy actor Rogers

40 One of the *Little Women*

41 "Bobby Shaftoe went to ____"

43 "Little pig" digits

45 "Peace ____ and mercy mild . . .": 2 words

48 Pain from a bee

52 ____ the tail on the donkey

53 Built or produced

55 Opera melody

56 Play a role in a play

57 Spoken, like some book reports

58 Quiet; peaceful

59 Nickname for Lester

60 Beams of sunlight

61 Bobby Shaftoe wore "buckles at his ____"

Down

1 The largest continent

2 Sound of a big gong

3 Sedan or coupe

4 Unit of Boy or Girl Scouts

5 Pair

6 "____ to You" (party song): 2 words

7 Always

8 "Three ____ a tub . . .": 2 words

9 Cake's party companion: 2 words

10 Not any

11 Opposite of subtracts

19 Word used to forbid actions

21 At this moment

23 ____ and order

25 Opposite of no

26 Creative work

27 Party gifts

30 "The Queen of Hearts, ____ made some tarts . . ."

31 Chasing game

34 Soft sound of a dove

35 Holes in needles

(Continued)

38 What the princess felt under her mattress

42 Knight's protection

44 Large pile of hay

45 October's birthstone

46 "Have a ____ day!"

47 Scarlett O'Hara's plantation

49 Modern-day Persia

50 Egypt's great river

51 Party entertainment like musical chairs

54 Elevated trains, for short

21.
Secret Messages
by Merryl Maleska

1. Here's a sentence that is written in code. To solve the secret message, you must go back one letter in the alphabet each time. For example, every B in the code becomes A and every C becomes B. The same idea is used throughout the alphabet. Can you solve the message?

BMM XPSL BOE OP QMBZ

NBLFT KBDL B EVMM CPZ

2. In this message, C becomes A and D becomes B, etc. In other words, go back two letters each time.

GZRGTKGPEG KU VJG

DGUV VGCEJGT

43

22.
The Crossword Code
by Merryl Maleska

Dr. Jones, who liked to make up crossword puzzles, was slowly poisoned in his den. Before he died, he pretended he was making a puzzle, but he was really leaving a coded message for the police.

U	I	F		C	V	U	M	F	S
X	B	T		U	I	F	P	O	F
X	I	P		L	J	M	M	F	E
N	F		I	F	I	B	U	F	E
N	F		B	O	E		I	F	
		Q	V	U					
U	I	F		Q	P	J	T	P	O
J	O		N	Z		X	J	O	F
I	F		J	T		I	F	S	F
X	B	U	D	I	J	O	H		
N	F				H	S	P	X	
		X	F	B	L	F	S		
B	O	E		X	F	B	L	F	S
B	S	S	F	T	U		I	J	N
G	P	S		N	V	S	E	F	S

The killer looked at the puzzle and thought that Dr. Jones had lost his senses because of the poison. But a smart detective realized that it was a secret message, and he broke the code.

You can solve the message, too,
if you use one of the two
directions on page 43.
We won't tell you which one.
Now fill in the blank diagram
with the correct letters.

T	h	e		B	u	t	l	e	r
W	a	s		T	h	e	o	n	e
w	h	o		k	i	l	l	e	d
m	e		h	e	h	a	t	e	d
m	e		a	n	d		h	e	
		p	u	t					
t	h	e		p	o	i	s	o	n
i	n		m	y		w	i	n	e
h	e		i	s		h	e	r	e
W	a	t	c	h	i	n	g		
m	e				g	r	o	w	
		w	e	a	k	e	r		
a	n	d		w	e	a	k	e	r
a	r	r	e	s	t		h	i	m
f	o	r		M	u	r	d	e	r.

45

23.
Allhallows Eve
by Caroline G. Fitzgerald

Across

1 Trick or ____!

6 Kind of sugar, syrup, or tree

11 Broom rider

12 Foreign or strange

13 TV actor Ed

14 "Jack ____ could eat no fat . . ."

15 The Red ____ is in Asia

16 Type or sort

18 Gorilla

19 Ex-champ Muhammad

20 Mix with a spoon

21 Night of October 31

24 Part of Superman's costume

25 ____-picking (being very fussy)

46

26 A part of your mouth

27 Suffix with steward

28 As white ___ ghost: 2 words

31 A homeless cat's "home"

33 "Peter, Peter, Pumpkin ___ . . ."

35 Actor-comedian Martin

36 Candy has a ___ taste

37 Companions of ladders on firetrucks

38 Years from 13 to 19

Down

1 "___ the night before Christmas . . . "

2 Get up or go up

3 Famed volcano of Sicily

4 Highest card

5 Shiver with excitement

6 Disguise for a ragamuffin

7 Swiss mountain

8 His costume has an eye patch

9 "___ lizards!" (Little Orphan Annie's cry)

10 Opposite of exit

17 Kings of the jungle

19 Beer-like beverage

20 Masqueraders may wait for the sun to ___

21 "___ the Chief" (presidential song): 2 words

22 Treats sometimes candied

23 Most learned

24 Loud, harsh metallic noise

27 What spectacles cover

28 Fit to ___ (suit exactly): 2 words

29 Viewed

30 ___ and crafts

32 Adam's wife

34 Mixture of fear and wonder

24.
Space Trip
by Vaughan Keith

¹	²	³	■	⁴	⁵	⁶	■	⁷	⁸	⁹	¹⁰

Across

1 Aide at the North Pole

4 Forbid

7 TV program about doctors in the war

11 Atmosphere

12 Stone, Iron, and Middle followers

14 Type of code

15 The Boston ____ Party

16 Bide one's time

17 ____ and cons

18 Inventor of the telescope

21 Three strikes, in baseball

22 604, in Caesar's day

24 By a whisker

26 Christmas

27 Film spool

28 Biblical garden

29 I love (Latin)

30 Part of the human eye

34 Opposite of "guys"

36 Heating duct

37 Faults or bad marks

41 Relatives of the moose

42 Hatchet

43 Planet closest to the sun

45 Crimson and scarlet

47 Average

48 Two words at a wedding

51 Journey

52 ____, crackle, and pop

53 Holy sister

54 Remain

55 Scientists' units of weight (Abbreviation)

56 Gosh!

Down

1 Dine

2 Untruth

3 Breakable

4 Cry loudly

5 Once more

6 First man on the moon: 2 words

7 Chart for a navigator

8 Archer's weapon

9 Capital of South Korea

10 Rapid

13 Music lover's purchase

19 Get even for a wrong

20 Neighbor of Wash. and Cal. (Abbreviation)

22 Coloring for clothes

23 What a cow chews

25 ____ Twist, Dickens hero

29 Visitors from outer space

31 Depending

32 Contents of a pen

33 Abbreviation for certain roads

35 Equip, as with a weapon

37 Popular game in English pubs

38 Use muscle power

39 Television, newspapers, and radio

40 Beat it!

44 Baseball officials, for short

46 Secret agent

49 Expected, as a homework assignment or a train

50 Half a couple

25.
Word Chain
by Merryl Maleska

In this puzzle the last letter of one word is the first letter of the next. Use the clues to fill in words. Then when you have finished the puzzle, write each numbered letter on a numbered blank to answer this question: What does "E.T." stand for?

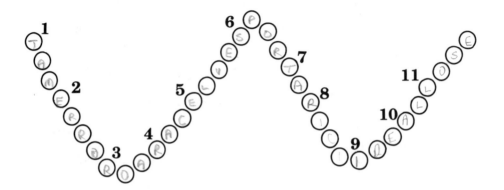

1 Not wild

2 A mistake

3 A lion's sound

4 What the hare and the tortoise ran

5 More than one elf

6 Baseball is one

7 This is used to pave highways and roofs

8 _____ -tikki-tavi is a mongoose in Kipling's *Jungle Book*

9 "Whose _____ was it to go swimming?"

10 Everybody

11 Opposite of win

Answer: EXTRA-

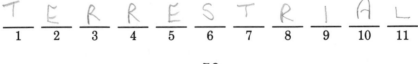

T	E	R	R	E	S	T	R	I	A	L
1	2	3	4	5	6	7	8	9	10	11

26.
Anagrams Game

by Susan Brown

An anagram is a word made by mixing up the letters in another word. For instance, MALE and LAME are anagrams for MEAL.

Across

1 Little lie

4 Marshy area

9 An anagram for waist

14 High card

15 Tag

16 *Little Orphan* ____

17 A flag color

18 Number of years one has lived

19 Not difficult

21 Do, ____, mi

22 An anagram for star or arts

24 School subject, for short

25 Senator Kennedy's nickname

26 Household job

28 An anagram for aces

29 "____ in Boots"

30 Owl's cry

31 An anagram for shoe

32 Evergreen tree

33 An anagram for ram

34 Opposite of light

35 Main meal of the day

38 Part of the verb "to be"

39 Farm building

40 An anagram for rots

41 ____ and behold

42 Album item

44 An anagram for nape

45 Was first

46 An anagram for tan

47 Bundle of hay

48 An anagram for care

49 An anagram for kale or leak

51 Stop

52 An anagram for point

53 An anagram for pea

54 An anagram for past, spat, or taps

51

(Continued)

55 An anagram for span or pans

56 Opposite of down

57 Where the sun rises

58 Move like a bunny

59 An anagram for sit

62 Drinking vessel

64 Not tight

66 An anagram for ton

67 Assists

68 Go in

69 Merry

Down

1 Opposite of near

2 Frozen water

3 Sleeping chamber

4 An anagram for stale, least, or tales

5 Moves like a dog's tail

6 Honest ____ (President Lincoln)

7 Myself

8 Polite word

9 Bathe

10 "Have you ____ wool?"

11 *The Cat ____ the Hat* by Dr. Seuss

12 An anagram for rites

13 Morsels for a bird

20 An anagram for tea or eat

23 An anagram for tar or rat

24 Part of a Halloween costume

25 An anagram for runt

26 Place to sit

27 An anagram for shore or hoers

28 Yellow vegetable

29 Two cups = one ____

31 Difficult

32 An arsonist starts it

34 Small arrow

35 Completed

36 Vote into office

37 Wild West show

39 Treat for a dog

40 An anagram for last

43 Birthday treat

44 An anagram for slap or Alps

45 Capital of Michigan

47 ____ of Gettysburg: 1863

48 Tear

49 Show amusement

50 Kind of fruit

51 Owns

52 Material made from wood pulp

54 An anagram for saps

55 Organ of smell

57 Sixth sense (Abbreviation)

58 Very warm

60 Fit ____ tee (suit exactly): 2 words

61 Pig's home

27.
Compound Words
by Mark Diehl

A compound word is one that is made up of two or more smaller words, such as: rowboat, quarterback, or kickstand. In this puzzle all of the answers are compound words. The clues are in two parts. First, a clue is given for the compound word as a whole; then in parentheses are clues for the words that form the compound word. Here is an example:

Roadside ad (duck's beak + piece of wood)
BILLBOARD   BILL   +   BOARD

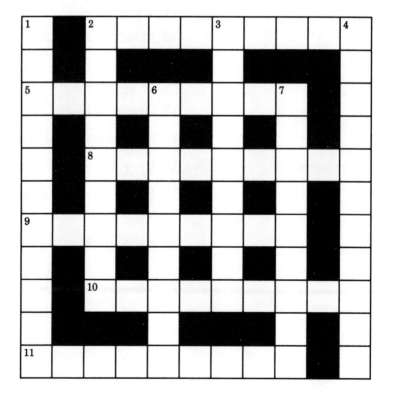

Across

2 Rowdy person (like sandpaper + area under your chin)

5 Falls, like a plane (what a dog wags + revolves)

8 Chinese eating utensil (use an ax + twig or cane)

9 Poisonous plant (frog's relative + seat with no back)

10 Fine pottery (rock + man-made items)

11 Pool wear (dog paddle + business clothes)

Down

1 Rabbits (soft material + opposite of heads)

2 Waterproof clothing (shower + jackets)

3 Icy chunk of rain (call a cab + pebble)

4 Foolish person (finger joint + chief)

6 Winter walking wear (fluffy frozen water + foot coverings)

7 Cargoes (schooner + burdens)

28.
What Do You Know?

by Walter Covell

Across

1 Shoulder-to-wrist area

4 On

8 Saucy

12 Scare word

13 African country

14 Thought

15 Young boy

16 Body covering

17 Barge pushers

18 Home of Adam and Eve

20 *Uncle Tom's Cabin* girl

21 Command to kitty

22 Dog-powered snow vehicle

24 Cooks are also called ch____

26 Ginger ____ is a sparkling drink

27 Summer or winter, for instance

29 ____ Williams was a famous baseball player

30 Melted ice

32 Dressing gowns

34 Beat the other team

35 Shooting star

37 Oil paintings, for instance

38 ____ Paolo, Brazil

39 Computer information

42 Penciled a picture

44 Bear's baby

46 Related or narrated

48 Have supper

49 Of the mouth

51 Also

52 Loaned

53 Say no

54 ____ Arbor, Michigan

55 Ages

56 Rim

57 Hip-to-ankle area

Down

1 Having ability enough

2 Streets or highways

3 Girl in a fashion show

4 Forenoons (Abbreviation)

5 Seize; capture

6 Pimentos might be used to stuff these fruits

7 Sleeveless dress

8 Deep holes

9 Instruct

10 Provides a feast for

11 Sampled the flavor of

19 Sparrow's home

23 Considers

25 Hairnet

28 First three digits in a telephone number: 2 words

30 One who feels anxious

31 Television tower

33 Spoiled child

34 Walk like a duck

36 Took a trip

40 Sum

41 Solo

43 Dampens

45 Gun sound

47 Ding ____ (bell sound)

50 It's found in some soaps

29.
Circle the Words: Colors

by James and Phyllis Barrick

The 35 words in the word list are hidden in the mixture of letters. The words can read forward or backward, up or down, or diagonally, but are always in a straight line. To complete the puzzle, locate each hidden word and draw a circle around it. A letter can appear in more than one word, so some of the circles you draw may cross or overlap. As you find the words, cross them off the list. When you have circled all of the words on the list, you have solved the puzzle.

```
A  U  V  E  O  G  I  D  N  I  S  T  U  R  Q
B  L  L  E  M  E  R  A  L  D  O  N  C  E  T
Q  U  N  J  R  A  K  L  T  C  A  N  A  E  R
A  I  P  E  S  M  N  C  I  E  L  W  L  C  E
W  H  I  T  E  W  I  R  R  A  L  O  I  U  C
I  M  O  B  O  R  P  L  V  I  I  R  L  P  E
V  I  L  L  A  A  G  E  I  V  M  B  A  T  R
O  H  L  A  T  A  N  E  S  O  R  S  U  C  I
R  E  E  C  N  D  I  O  V  E  N  R  O  E  S
Y  E  G  K  E  R  K  D  D  I  Q  L  I  N  E
A  G  I  R  G  A  C  W  L  U  L  M  M  O  V
C  N  E  T  A  L  O  C  O  H  C  O  H  O  U
E  A  B  S  M  P  H  I  G  U  F  D  E  R  A
O  R  E  V  L  I  S  A  F  F  R  O  N  A  M
C  O  R  A  L  E  L  P  R  U  P  U  Q  M  I
```

Apricot, beige, brown, cerise, chocolate, coral, crimson, emerald, gold, indigo, ivory, jet black, lavender, lilac, magenta, maroon, mauve, olive green, orange, powder blue, puce, purple, red, rose, saffron, scarlet, sepia, shocking pink, silver, tan, turquoise, vermilion, violet, white, yellow.

30.
Making Sense Out of Nonsense

by Merryl Maleska

These nonsense words are each made up of two words that are synonyms for the two words in a real compound word. For example, "belowsteps" is a made-up synonym for "downstairs." Find the matching compound word in the box below and write it next to its "synonym." (Be careful: Not all words in the box will be used.)

1 houseill   _homesick_

2 flamespot   _fireplace_

3 starglow   _sunlight_

4 cotcell   _bedroom_

5 lawnjumper   _grasshopper_

6 stormjacket   _raincoat_

7 greatmom   _grandmother_

8 belowsea   _underwater_

9 behindsoil   _background_

10 tireseat   _wheelchair_

grasshopper	homesick	newspaper
cowboy	sunlight	grandmother
wheelchair	headache	bedroom
underwater	fireplace	bookstore
raincoat	background	birthday

31.
Weather Report
by Vaughan Keith

Across

1 Half of a quartet

4 Walter Mondale's party (Abbreviation)

7 Jason's ship (used to get the Golden Fleece)

11 "____ the land of the free . . ."

12 Anger

13 Cirrocumulus, for example

14 *Homo sapiens*

15 Weatherman's aid in space

17 Mode of transport for a witch

19 Make corrections, as for a newspaper article

20 Where some clouds float

25 Smear; make hazy

26 "Snow White and the ____ Dwarfs"

27 Opposite of fore, at sea

30 Summit

32 Humpty-Dumpty was one

33 Tartan

36 Tardy

39 Weather alert: 2 words

43 Steep, rugged cliff

44 Take it easy

46 This goes with thunder

50 Yours and mine

51 Units of land, as on a farm

52 Take to court

53 Important material in genes: Initials

54 Insects living in hives

55 Material used by blasters

56 Where pigs wallow

Down

1 Grant's ____ is in New York City

2 Has on

3 "Believe It ____," by Ripley: 2 words

4 Bleak, like a rainy day

5 Historical period of time

6 Weatherman

7 "____ king's horses . . .": 2 words

8 King: French

9 Destroy the interior, as by fire

10 Kind of poem

13 Cuts or football fouls

16 TV's Sullivan and Asner

18 Every planet is an ____

21 Famous Pharaoh, for short

22 New Year's ____

23 Normal (Abbreviation)

24 Course in school (Abbreviation)

27 Likely

28 Character on *Alice*

29 Road covering

31 Rabbit's foot

34 A foot has twelve of these

35 Popular board game

37 Bull's-eye

38 Summer in France

40 Cupid's first name

(Continued)

41 Oafs

42 Some people believe that ghosts ____ houses

45 Doctor's "photograph"

46 Where chemists work, for short

47 What glaciers are partly made of

48 Rain helps to make the grass stay ____en

49 Woman living in a convent

32.
Hidden Animal Hunt

by Louis Sabin

There are 63 animals in the word-cage. How many can you find? Read up, down, left to right, right to left, and diagonally. To give you a start, "zoo" has already been circled.

33.
The Orchestra
by Alfio Micci

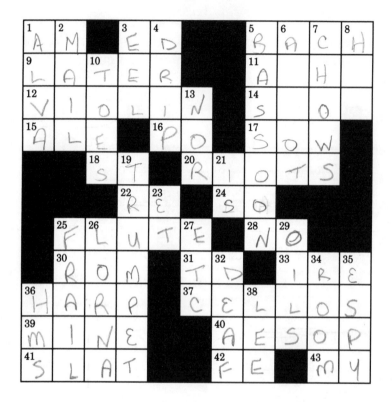

Across

1 Opposite of P.M.

3 Editor (Abbreviation)

5 Great German composer

9 "See you ____, alligator!"

11 Tennis star Arthur

12 Stringed instrument

14 Boat that carries garbage

15 Brew

16 Post office (Abbreviation)

17 Female pig

18 ____ Patrick is the patron of Ireland (Abbreviation)

20 Uprisings by mobs

22 Do, ____, mi

24 Fa, ____, la

25 Wind instrument with many holes

28 "Jack Sprat could eat ____ fat"

30 Julius Caesar was a ____an leader

31 Football score (Abbreviation)

33 Wrath

36 Stringed instrument

37 Stringed instruments

39 Where to find ore

40 Fable writer

41 Venetian-blind part

42 Santa ____, New Mexico

43 ____ *Fair Lady* is a famous musical comedy or movie

Down

1 Edison's middle name

2 What the postman brings

3 Slippery fish

4 Person resembling a twerp or a nerd

5 Wind instrument

6 Necktie

7 Dogs that originally came from China

8 This means "chop" and sounds like "you"

10 "Bells on her ____"

13 Partner of neither

19 Brass instrument

21 A trombone ____ a musical instrument

23 A clarin____ is a woodwind instrument

25 Not strong

26 ____ *Doone* is a famous book

27 And so forth (Abbreviation)

29 Greases

32 Unable to hear

34 What you pay for in a motel

35 Catch sight of

36 ____ *Pinafore* is a comic opera by Gilbert and Sullivan

38 Southern general

34.
Animalgrams
by Mark Diehl

The letters of A + ROB can be rearranged to spell the animal: BOAR. What animals, wild or otherwise, can be made by unscrambling the following pairs of letters and words? A score of 20 is excellent!

1 A + GLEE = eagle
2 B + CAR = crab
3 C + BOAR = cobra
4 D + OAT = toad
5 E + RED = deer
6 F + LOW = wolf
7 G + RITE = tiger
8 H + SORE = horse
9 I + BORN = robin
10 J + ALACK = jackal
11 K + RASH = shark
12 L + UTTER = turtle
13 M + LACE = camel

14 N + SAKE = snake
15 O + SOME = moose
16 P + RELOAD =
17 U + MAP = puma
18 R + COW = crow
19 S + LAIN =
20 T + AGO = goat
21 U + TAN =
22 V + DOE = dove
23 W + HEAL = whale
24 X + ONE =
25 Y + STORE =
26 Z + BEAR = zebra

35.
A Real Challenger

by A. J. Santora

Across

1 On Christmas Eve, some people go to Midnight ___

5 "The Raven" author

8 Turkish title

13 That ___ say: 2 words

14 Look at with desire

(Continued)

16 Speak without notes

17 TV cartoon show: 2 words

19 Gullible; innocent

20 From head to ____

21 Abbreviation for Dublin's land

22 Stumbled

24 Calm

26 Straight up

27 Word with cent or capita

28 Mrs. Reagan, for short

29 Soft drink

33 Bustling about

36 Saint whose feast day is January 21

38 Detective, for short

39 Mrs. Wiggs' place for dolls?: 3 words

42 "____ the land of the free"

43 A size of pizza or coke

44 Draw forth

45 What some dolls say

47 Charlotte of *Facts of Life* on TV

48 Hawaiian garland

49 Winnie and others

51 Most strange

55 Popular rock singer

58 Letters of a debtor

59 What you need to breathe

60 Some exams

61 One of the Muppets: 2 words

64 Ending for Evans or Anderson or many other cities

65 Bargain event

66 Opponents of Reps. (Abbreviation)

67 Writer T.S. or George

68 "Three ____ in a tub"

69 Smell ____ (suspect): 2 words

Down

1 Catchers' gloves

2 " . . . an old lady who lived in ____": 2 words

3 Beef cattle

4 Distress call (initials)

5 Fountain worker, sometimes

6 Bogeyman

7 Santa's helper

8 Push the ____ button (get alarmed)

9 Fits to suit

10 Small error

11 Bee's place

12 Life isn't ____ of roses!: 2 words

15 Cause to become aloof

18 Animal, vegetable, or ____

23 Actress Taylor

25 Heroic poem

26 Hires

30 Beetle Bailey's dog

31 On ____ (ready to bat)

32 Throb

33 Small particle that's very powerful

34 Mets' stadium

35 Semester

36 Lincoln's namesakes

37 Advance the pace: 2 words

40 The Red ____ in *Peanuts*

41 Zealous

46 Handsome youth or Greek god

48 Untie a knot

50 Beginning

52 Kind of beaver

53 Greek letter used by many fraternities

54 Meet in secret

55 Relocate

56 Seed covering

57 Painter Salvador

58 ____ of Capri

62 "____ an American": 2 words

63 Rhoda's mother on TV or actress Lupino

Answers

1

I		II
A	CAB	CAFE
ACE	CAD	DEAF
AD	DAB	FA
ADE	BADE	FACE
BAD	BEAD	FAD
BE	DACE	FADE
BED	(a fish)	FED

2

M	O	M		H	I	S		M	A	Y
A	L	I		A	C	E		A	D	E
D	E	C		R	E	C	O	R	D	S
		K	I	D		R	O	Y		
E	Y	E	S		P	E	P	P	E	R
B	O	Y		P	A	T		O	W	E
B	U	M	P	E	R		S	P	E	D
	O	U	T		P	O	P			
S	T	U	T	T	E	R		I	T	S
S	I	S		E	V	E		N	O	T
T	E	E		D	A	Y		S	P	Y

3

A	P	E		S	I	R		A	N	T
S	I	X		I	R	E		T	O	N
P	E	P		M	I	S	T	E	R	T
	L	O	O	S	E	R				
L	E	A	R	N		T	I	M	I	D
E	R	I	E			V	A	L	E	
G	A	N	G	S		G	I	R	L	S
		O	P	E	R	A	S			
G	R	A	N	O	L	A		H	A	M
O	I	L		I	S	T		A	G	E
O	D	E		L	E	E		L	O	T

4

S	T	O	R	M	Y		C	R	E	A	M	Y
	O		U					O			U	
M	O	M	M	Y				O			M	
M		M		Y		A	R	M	Y		M	
Y		Y				C		Y			Y	
Y		S	W		A							P
U		A	O		D			J	I	M	M	Y
M		M	R		E							G
M		M	M		M							M
Y		Y	Y		Y		E	N	E	M	Y	

5

I	R	I	S		A	H	E	M
T	A	K	E		M	O	V	E
C	R	E	A	M		N	E	T
H	E			I	C	E	R	
		C	A	N	D	Y		
	C	O	S	T			T	I
P	A	N		S	U	G	A	R
U	K	E	S		S	U	C	K
N	E	S	T		A	M	O	S

6

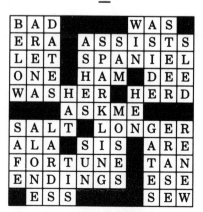

B	A	D				W	A	S	
E	R	A		A	S	S	I	S	T	S
L	E	T		S	P	A	N	I	E	L
O	N	E		H	A	M		D	E	E
W	A	S	H	E	R		H	E	R	D
			A	S	K	M	E			
S	A	L	T		L	O	N	G	E	R
A	L	A		S	I	S		A	R	E
F	O	R	T	U	N	E		T	A	N
E	N	D	I	N	G	S		E	S	E
	E	S	S					S	E	W

7

```
M A M A . . M A P .
O V E R . W A T E R S
T O N E . A N . S E T
H I . . A G O . T A R
. D A N C E R . D A .
. R A T S . C H E W .
. R A M S . D O O R .
T U B E . C A L M . .
O N . T A S T E S . .
A N T . A S H . T O .
S E E . M E . S H O P
T R A D E S . H I V E
. . R O D . E D E N .
```

8

```
A W A Y . E A S T
T A P E . S L U R
E R E . P E A C E
. A R E . . H E .
C H R I S T M A S
L O . T O A . . .
A U T O S . R E D
U S E D . S I L O
S E N D . T A F T
```

9

1. Angel
2. Angle
3. Ankle
4. Anger
5. Dance
6. Candy
7. Panda
8. Canal
9. Stand
10. Chant
11. Grand
12. Piano
13. Clean
14. Pecan
15. Sedan
16. Organ
17. Alien
18. Asian
19. Again
20. Apron

10

11

					FRUITS:
FG	IR	AN	DP	EI	GRAPE
AN	GP	OP	LN	EL	APPLE
BY	EH	AR	LR	FY	BERRY
AL	EW	MO	OR	MN	LEMON
PT	EH	AE	CR	EH	PEACH

Riddle: What is worse than finding a worm in your apple?

Finding only half a worm there

71

12

S	O	N	S			I	N	S			A	J	A	R
E	D	I	T			N	E	T			S	U	R	E
L	O	N	E			T	A	R			A	M	E	N
F	R	E	E	Z	E	T	A	G			P	A	T	
			R	O	N			P	A	I	R			
C	A	R			O	D	D			S	T	O	R	E
A	L	E	S			S	A	M			S	P	U	N
W	I	D	E	R			Y	E	T			E	G	G
			R	E	A	P			A	I	M			
F	R	O			H	O	P	S	C	O	T	C	H	
L	A	V	A			I	O	U			T	A	L	E
A	G	E	D			N	O	R			E	X	A	M
W	E	R	E			T	H	E			L	I	P	S

13

A	C	I	D			S	E	N	D			R	E	D
R	O	D	E			E	V	E	R			A	D	E
T	W	O	S			P	E	T	E			G	E	E
				K	I	T				S	P	E	N	D
R	O	A	S	T			B	A	S	E				
E	G	G			E	P	I	C			N	I	C	E
A	R	E			M	E	L	T	S			R	O	N
P	E	S	T			A	L	S	O			O	D	D
			E	A	S	Y			A	N	N	E	S	
S	A	L	A	D				I	K	E				
I	R	E			A	C	E	S			E	R	I	E
T	E	N			M	O	A	N			D	I	L	L
S	A	D			S	O	R	T			Y	O	L	K

14

O	A	T	H			S	O	F	T			P	A	T
F	L	E	A			T	R	I	O			A	D	E
F	E	A	R			O	G	R	E			N	U	N
			D	I	V	A	S			L	I	L	T	
S	I	S			D	E	N	T			A	C	T	S
S	T	I	L	L			S	L	O	T				
E	S	T	E	E	M			Y	A	C	H	T	S	
			D	R	I	P			S	H	A	R	E	
F	L	O	G			R	I	D	E			D	Y	E
L	O	P	E			A	R	O	S	E				
A	Y	E			S	C	A	N			S	T	A	Y
M	A	N			A	L	T	O			A	I	D	E
E	L	S			D	E	E	R			U	P	O	N

15

```
                B A N K
      H U L A
                S H O U T
    C H I M E
                B L A C K
      S A N T A
                L I B R A R Y
    T R A V E L
                G L A D
        S E A
                M O U S E
    G L O V E
```

16

C	A	P	E			H	A	L	T			A	B	E
O	P	E	N			E	R	I	E			R	E	D
W	E	N	T			A	M	E	N			T	A	G
			E	N	D			T	A	S	T	E		
S	T	O	R	E			V	A	S	T				
T	O	N			S	L	O	B			E	D	E	N
A	R	E			T	I	T	L	E			A	X	E
R	E	S	T			F	E	E	L			R	A	W
			E	A	T	S			S	T	E	M	S	
T	O	T	A	L			B	E	E					
A	H	A			T	I	M	E			A	G	E	S
R	I	M			A	C	E	S			R	O	V	E
T	O	E			R	E	N	T			S	T	E	W

17

18

A	B	C	D		E	F	G	H		I	J	K
R	E	A	R		A	R	E	A		V	A	N
E	D	N	A		R	Y	E	S		A	D	O
			G	A	S			T	E	N	E	T
G	R	O	S	S		O	P	E	N			
R	A	M		K	A	T	E		D	A	R	T
A	G	E		S	I	T	E	S		S	E	A
B	E	N	T		M	E	R	E		I	N	G
			U	S	S	R		C	O	A	T	S
B	O	U	G	H			I	T	S			
A	L	P		A	M	E	N		C	O	L	A
L	E	O		F	O	L	K		A	R	I	D
D	O	N		T	O	M	S		R	E	E	D

19

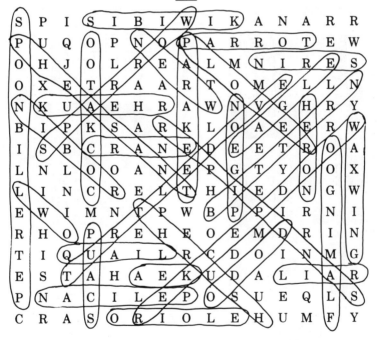

Auk, bittern, cockatoo, crane, dodo, eagle, flamingo, heron, ibis, kea, kiwi, meadowlark, oriole, owl, parakeet, parrot, pelican, petrel, pheasant, pigeon, plover, quail, rail, rhea, robin, sandpiper, scaup, serin, sparrow, spoonbill, thrush, turtledove, waxwing, woodpecker, wren.

20

A	B	A	T		T	H	E	M		I	N	A
S	O	U	R		W	A	V	E		C	O	D
I	N	T	O		O	P	E	N		E	N	D
A	G	O	O	D		P	R	I	N	C	E	S
		P	O	L	Y		N	O	R			
Y	A	P		N	A	B		W	E	S	T	
E	R	R		T	W	I	C	E		A	H	A
S	T	E	P		R	O	Y		M	E	G	
	S	E	A		T	O	E	S				
O	N	E	A	R	T	H		S	T	I	N	G
P	I	N		M	A	D	E		A	R	I	A
A	C	T		O	R	A	L		C	A	L	M
L	E	S		R	A	Y	S		K	N	E	E

21

1. All work and no play makes Jack a dull boy.
2. Experience is the best teacher.

22

T	H	E		B	U	T	L	E	R
W	A	S		T	H	E	O	N	E
W	H	O		K	I	L	L	E	D
M	E		H	E	H	A	T	E	D
M	E		A	N	D		H	E	
	P	U	T						
T	H	E		P	O	I	S	O	N
I	N		M	Y		W	I	N	E
H	E		I	S		H	E	R	E
W	A	T	C	H	I	N	G		
M	E			G	R	O	W		
	W	E	A	K	E	R			
A	N	D		W	E	A	K	E	R
A	R	R	E	S	T		H	I	M
F	O	R		M	U	R	D	E	R

23

T	R	E	A	T		M	A	P	L	E
W	I	T	C	H		A	L	I	E	N
A	S	N	E	R		S	P	R	A	T
S	E	A		I	L	K		A	P	E
		A	L	I		S	T	I	R	
	H	A	L	L	O	W	E	E	N	
C	A	P	E		N	I	T			
L	I	P		E	S	S		A	S	A
A	L	L	E	Y		E	A	T	E	R
S	T	E	V	E		S	W	E	E	T
H	O	S	E	S		T	E	E	N	S

The butler was the one who killed me. He hated me and he put the poison in my wine. He is here watching me grow weaker and weaker. Arrest him for murder!

E	L	F	■	B	A	N	■	M	A	S	H
A	I	R	■	A	G	E	S	■	A	R	E	A
T	E	A	■	W	A	I	T	■	P	R	O	S
■	G	A	L	I	L	E	O	■	O	U	T
D	C	I	V	■	N	A	R	R	O	W	L	Y
Y	U	L	E	■	R	E	E	L	■
E	D	E	N	■	A	M	O	■	I	R	I	S
■	G	A	L	S	■	V	E	N	T
D	E	M	E	R	I	T	S	■	E	L	K	S
A	X	E	■	M	E	R	C	U	R	Y	■
R	E	D	S	■	N	O	R	M	■	I	D	O
T	R	I	P	■	S	N	A	P	■	N	U	N
S	T	A	Y	■	G	M	S	■	G	E	E

25

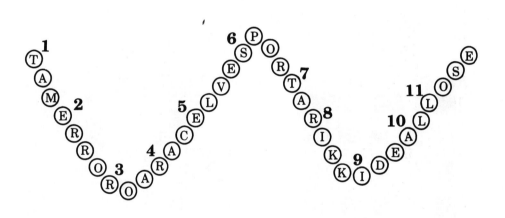

EXTRA-

$\underset{1}{T}\ \underset{2}{E}\ \underset{3}{R}\ \underset{4}{R}\ \underset{5}{E}\ \underset{6}{S}\ \underset{7}{T}\ \underset{8}{R}\ \underset{9}{I}\ \underset{10}{A}\ \underset{11}{L}$

```
F I B   S W A M P   W A I T S
A C E   L A B E L   A N N I E
R E D   A G E   E A S Y   R E
    R A T S   M A T H   T E D
C H O R E   C A S E   P U S S
H O O T   H O S E   F I R
A R M   D A R K   D I N N E R
I S   B A R N   S O R T   L O
R E C O R D   P A N E   L E D
    A N T   B A L E   R A C E
L A K E   H A L T   P I N T O
A P E   P A T S   N A P S
U P   E A S T   H O P   I T S
G L A S S   L O O S E   N O T
H E L P S   E N T E R   G A Y
```

```
C   R O U G H N E C K   K
O   A         A         N
T A I L S P I N S       U
T   N   N   L   H       C
O   C H O P S T I C K   L
N   O   W   T   P       E
T O A D S T O O L       H
A   T   H   N   O       H
I   S T O N E W A R E   E
L       E       D       A
S W I M S U I T S       D
```

```
A R M   A T O P   P E R T
B O O   M A L I   I D E A
L A D   S K I N   T U G S
E D E N   E V A   S C A T
  S L E D   E F S   A L E
    S E A S O N   T E D
  W A T E R   R O B E S
W O N   M E T E O R
A R T   S A O   D A T A
D R E W   C U B   T O L D
D I N E   O R A L   T O O
L E N T   D E N Y   A N N
E R A S   E D G E   L E G
```

29

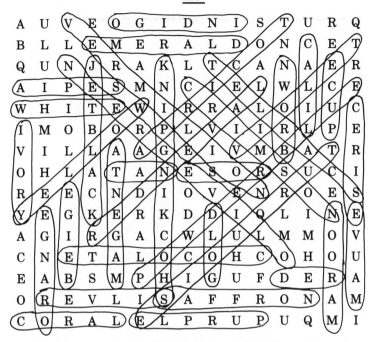

```
A  U  V  E  O  G  I  D  N  I  S  T  U  R  Q
B  L  L  E  M  E  R  A  L  D  O  N  C  E  T
Q  U  N  J  R  A  K  L  T  C  A  N  A  E  R
A  I  P  E  S  M  N  C  I  E  L  W  L  C  E
W  H  I  T  E  W  I  R  R  A  L  O  I  U  C
I  M  O  B  O  R  P  L  V  I  I  R  L  P  E
V  I  L  L  A  G  E  I  V  M  B  A  T  R  R
O  H  L  A  T  A  N  E  S  O  R  S  U  C  I
R  E  E  C  N  D  I  O  V  E  N  R  O  E  S
Y  E  G  K  E  R  K  D  D  I  Q  L  I  N  E
A  G  I  R  G  A  C  W  L  U  L  M  M  O  V
C  N  E  T  A  L  O  C  O  H  C  O  H  O  U
E  A  B  S  M  P  H  I  G  U  F  D  E  R  A
O  R  E  V  L  I  S  A  F  F  R  O  N  A  M
C  O  R  A  L  E  L  P  R  U  P  U  Q  M  I
```

Apricot, beige, brown, cerise, chocolate, coral, crimson, emerald, gold, indigo, ivory, jet black, lavender, lilac, magenta, maroon, mauve, olive green, orange, powder blue, puce, purple, red, rose, saffron, scarlet, sepia, shocking pink, silver, tan, turquoise, vermilion, violet, white, yellow.

30

1. homesick
2. fireplace
3. sunlight
4. bedroom
5. grasshopper
6. raincoat
7. grandmother
8. underwater
9. background
10. wheelchair

31

T	W	O		D	E	M			A	R	G	O
O	E	R		I	R	E		C	L	O	U	D
M	A	N		S	A	T	E	L	L	I	T	E
B	R	O	O	M		E	D	I	T			
	S	T	R	A	T	O	S	P	H	E	R	E
		B	L	U	R		S	E	V	E	N	
A	F	T		T	O	P		E	G	G		
P	L	A	I	D		L	A	T	E			
T	O	R	N	A	D	O	W	A	T	C	H	
		C	R	A	G		R	E	L	A	X	
L	I	G	H	T	N	I	N	G		O	U	R
A	C	R	E	S		S	U	E		D	N	A
B	E	E	S		T	N	T		S	T	Y	

32

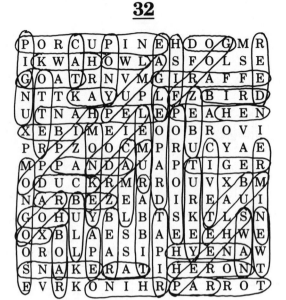

```
P O R C U P I N E H D O G M R
I K W A H O W L A S F O L S E
G O A T R N V M G I R A F F E
N T T K A Y U P L F Z B I R D
U T N A H P E L E P E A H E N
X E B I M E I E O O B R O V I
P R P Z O O C M P R U C Y A E
M P P A N D A U A P T I G E R
O D U C K R M R R O U V X B M
N A R B E Z E A D I R E A U I
G O H U Y B L B T S K T L S N
O X B L A E S B A E E E H W E
O R O L P A S I P H Y E N A W
S N A K E R A T I H E R O N T
F V R K O N I H R P A R R O T
```

Ape, bat, bear, bird, boa, boar, bull, camel, cat, civet, deer,
dog, duck, eagle, elephant, ermine, fish, frog, giraffe, gnu, goat,
goose, hawk, hen, heron, hippo, hog, hyena, ibex, lemur,
leopard, lion, mare, mongoose, monkey, mule, newt, otter, owl,
ox, panda, parr, parrot, peahen, pig, pony, porcupine,
porpoise, puma, rabbit, rat, reindeer, rhino, roo, sheep, snake,
swan, tapir, tiger, turkey, yak, zebra, zebu.

33

```
A M . E D . B A C H
L A T E R . A S H E
V I O L I N . S C O W
A L E . P O . S O W
. . S T . R I O T S
. . R E . S O . .
. F L U T E . N O .
. R O M . T D . I R E
H A R P . C E L L O S
M I N E . A E S O P
S L A T . F E . M Y
```

34

1. eagle		14. snake
2. crab		15. moose
3. cobra		16. leopard
4. toad		17. puma
5. deer		18. crow
6. wolf		19. snail
7. tiger		20. goat
8. horse		21. tuna
9. robin		22. dove
10. jackal		23. whale
11. shark		24. oxen
12. turtle		25. oyster
13. camel		26. zebra

M	A	S	S		P	O	E			P	A	S	H	A
I	S	T	O		O	G	L	E		A	D	L	I	B
T	H	E	S	M	U	R	F	S		N	A	I	V	E
T	O	E		I	R	E		T	R	I	P	P	E	D
S	E	R	E	N	E		E	R	E	C	T			
			P	E	R		N	A	N		S	O	D	A
A	S	T	I	R		A	G	N	E	S		T	E	C
T	H	E	C	A	B	B	A	G	E	P	A	T	C	H
O	E	R		L	A	R	G	E		E	V	O	K	E
M	A	M	A		R	A	E		L	E	I			
			P	O	O	H	S		O	D	D	E	S	T
M	A	D	O	N	N	A		I	O	U		A	I	R
O	R	A	L	S		M	I	S	S	P	I	G	G	Y
V	I	L	L	E		S	A	L	E		D	E	M	S
E	L	I	O	T			M	E	N		A	R	A	T